Rejected letter

Rejected letter

Evisa Isabella Rose

Special thanks to my sister, Laura,
for her help, love and support.

~About the book~

Rejected letter is an illustrated collection
of motivational aphorisms and poetry
about heartbreak, depression, trauma, love,
self-love and self-empowerment.
Feel angry or happy, sad or fearless!
Let your emotions flow.
Embrace them or release them...

★   ★   ★   ★   ★   ★   ★

~About the author~

Evisa Isabella Rose is an author, a comic strip
cartoonist, a photographer and an illustrator.
She describes herself as a bizarre mix
of a delicate soul, a curious mind, a thirsty
heart and a twisted sense of humor.

Contents

I refill my pen with pain...

A new war used to begin
every time she stared
at the vastness
of her empty notebook.

Intensity.
Agony.
And then: explosion!

You could find a piece of
her heart in every chapter.

Those pages were written
with a flaming quill.
Those velvet words
were embroidered with
eternal, golden thread...

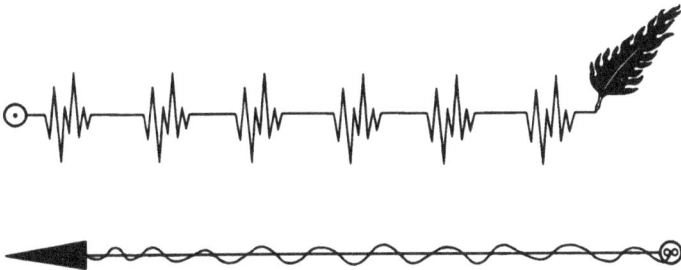

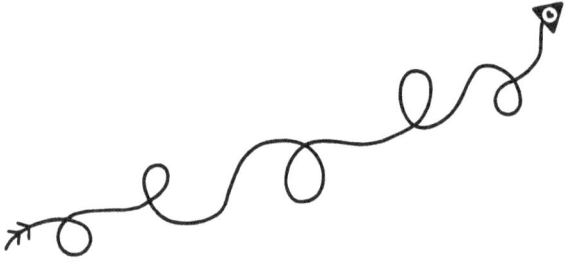

Life was so simple
before stepping into the complicated
trails of adulthood.

But I still keep
my young heart as a compass.
It always shows the right way
because it's pure...

Close your eyes and imagine.
Imagine the playful, rustling sound
of the wheat fields.

Do you remember when you were young
and all you needed was
a golden field and a blue sky?

And now you have grown up.
Lost between concrete boxes
and grey clouds.

Continuously and endlessly running.
But what are you running from?
Who is your invisible enemy?

Stop! Take a deep breath and
try remembering that kid.

That kid who didn't have much,
but had it all...

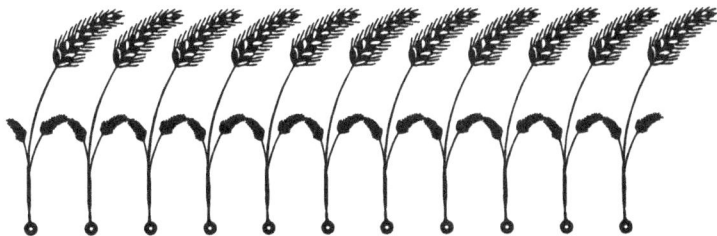

R.I.P.

Unconfessed
Feelings

R.I.P.

Unexpressed
Emotions

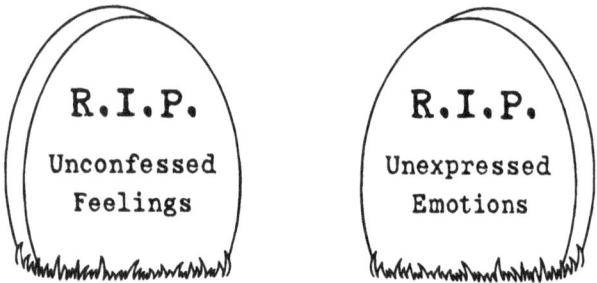

The knot of unspoken words
was slowly suffocating her...

She took the same train
she had been taking for years,
on the same route
she had been using for years
and went home,
inside the same boring walls
she had been hiding for years.

She had died,
even if she was still breathing...

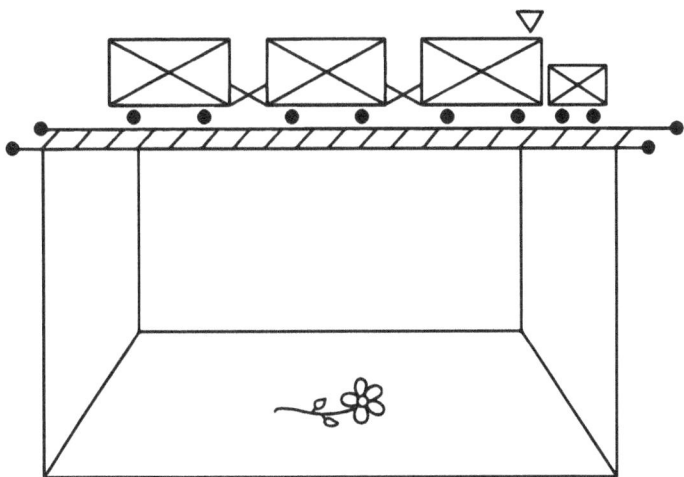

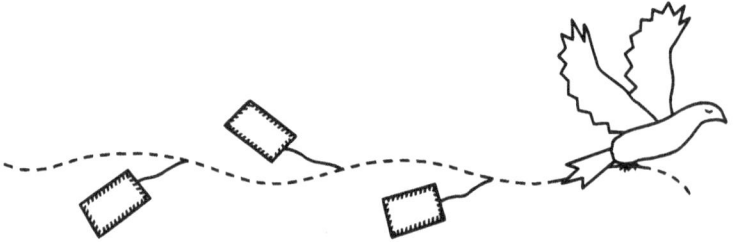

Whenever I try to rest,
the carrier pigeons of my mind
start bringing me illustrated
postcards of forgotten stories.

There I am again.
So carefree, so happy.
Happiness seems to be lost
in the frenetic pendulum of time now.

Happiness seems to be such an
old feeling these days...

There is no lifeguard here.
No one is going to save you
from drowning
in the turbulent whirl
of your dreadful thoughts.

You are the hero that you're looking for!

Now come back to the surface!
Come back before it's too late, darling!

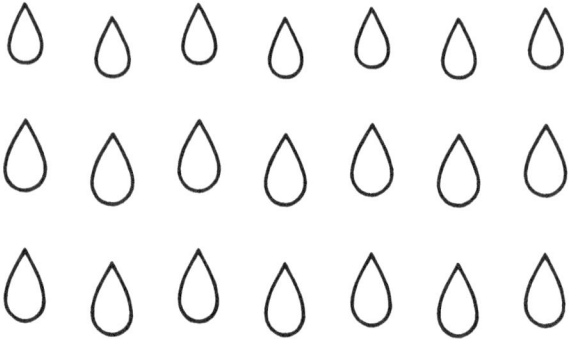

Don't hold your tears.
Let them run like magnificent waterfalls.
Let them take away
all the wicked pictures of yesterday.

And a refreshing tide will embrace
and calm their violent waters...

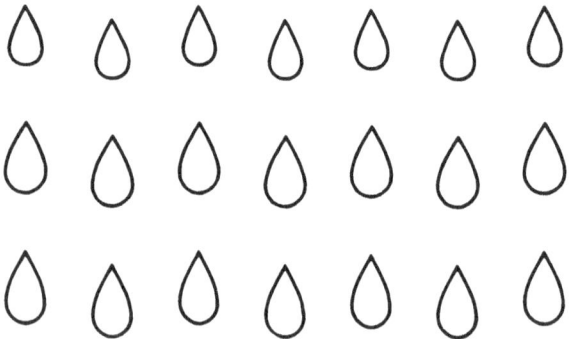

It has been too dark for too long.
And whenever I try to light my little candle,
the wind slithers inside my room
and blows it out,
again and again and again.

But then I look outside my window:
those tireless, twinkling stars
on an endless, black field of sky.

And a drip of foolish hope
calms my shivering heart.
Maybe one day they will come closer
and brighten my cold and gloomy room.

Maybe, maybe one day...

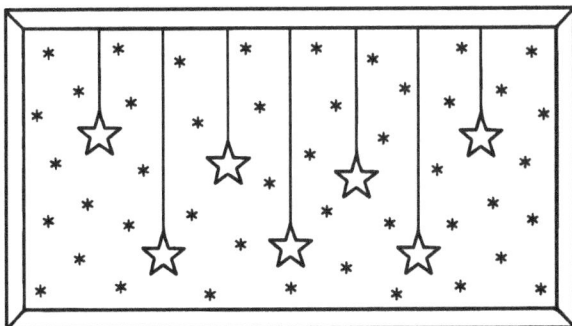

She was lost in a magical land
where Reality collided with Imagination
and the cheerful musical notes
of her Heart fought with
the strict voices of her Logic...

You feel like the world is against you.
You feel stuck.
You think you're running out of air,
but look closer in the mirror.
The hands around your neck are... yours.

Listen, kid!
Sometimes there are no enemies.
Sometimes the only enemy
you have to face is hidden between
the reflections of your mirror!

And he won't disappear if you
just decide to close your eyes.

No one can teach a bird how to fly
if it doesn't want to learn.
And your arms will never become wings
if you are afraid of
losing the ground under your feet!

I know you can do this
because I believe in you.
So, inhale a piece of courage and jump!

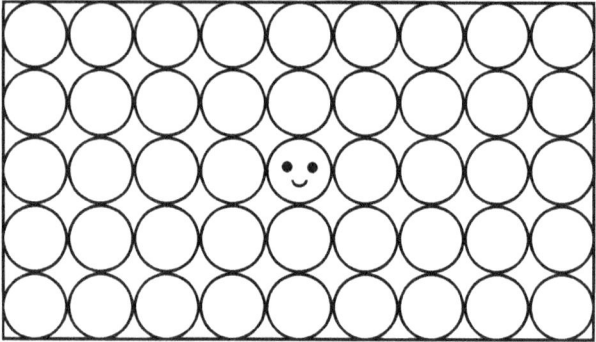

Full rooms have seen my smile.
Empty rooms have seen my tears...

Here she comes
Shining like the sun
Walking into the room
Hypnotizing everyone

She plays, she dances
She sings out loud
She is like a fairy
Flying all around

But if you could see
The truth behind her smile
You would feel that her heart
Hasn't been laughing for a while

And if you could see
The story behind her eyes
You would feel the pain
The pain from her scars

But she continues to smile
Like a shiny pearl
Oh, my poor
My poor little girl

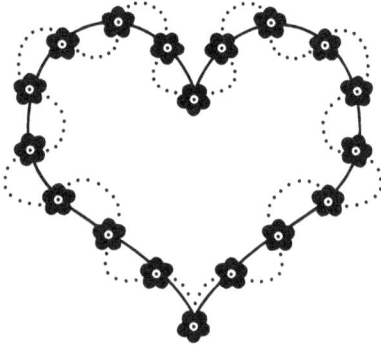

A heavy burden above my head.
A rough pathway under my feet.
But I can't quit, no I can't quit
as long as I have these
flower garlands in my heartbeat...

I knew the sky was blue for you,
but for me, its colors had vanished
by the cruel affliction of yesterday.

I was a curled up lifeless silhouette
fighting in a bed of thorns
against enormous, invisible monsters.

I was choking in their bitterness.
I had lost my appetite for the morning sun.
I was disappearing into a bottomless void
of obsessive thoughts.
I was praying for this chaotic,
inner turmoil to finally end.

But I couldn't give up.
I couldn't let them win so easily.
They were the disturbing, uninvited guests
who aggressively had entered my head
and were occupying vital space for free.

They were the vicious criminals
who had killed my life in cold blood
and had drawn disfigured feelings
through her walls without my permission.

*They were the ones who should leave,
not me!*

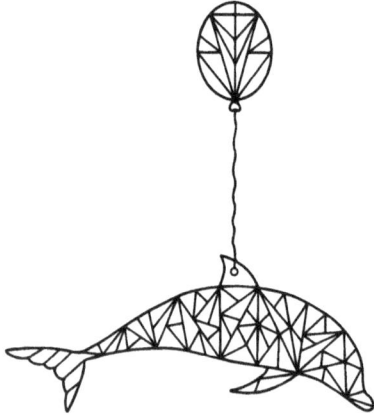

She was everything,
but he wanted anything.

So she left and he suddenly
remained with nothing.

In our lives
we take our paths.

Risky or safe,
easy or right.

The answers
are within us,
but few can see
truth's light!

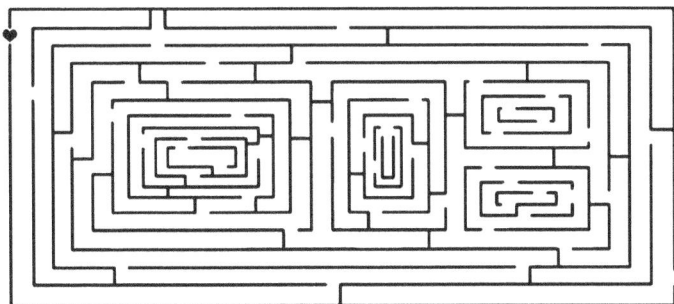

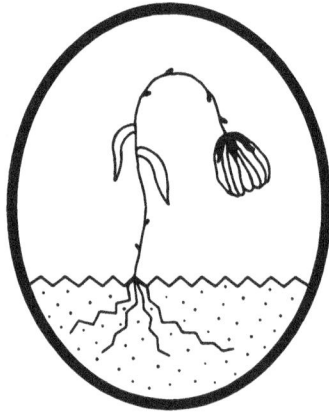

And you lost your future
by staying stuck in a wilted,
yet comfortable yesteryear...

A hostage of your past.
That's what you are.
It has tied your feet
in a pile of distorted memories
and you can't even make
a small step towards your future!

Don't expect me to rescue you.
I can't do it.
You are the only one
who can increase or weaken
the power of your old punisher.

Will you stay there
and miserably decompose
or will you cut those dusty ropes
and search for the gifts of tomorrow?

The main factors
that can change someone
for the better or for the worse are two:
love and the lack of love.

This elegant building
was standing proudly
and giving a joyful
breeze of life
to everyone around it,
when a traumatic strike
suddenly tore it down.

Don't push this ruined place
to immediately fix itself.

First, it needs
a little bit of understanding,
a little bit of compassion
and a little bit of love
to repair the sore fractures
of its happiness.

Carefully,
patiently,
quietly,
it will come back
even more exultant
than before!

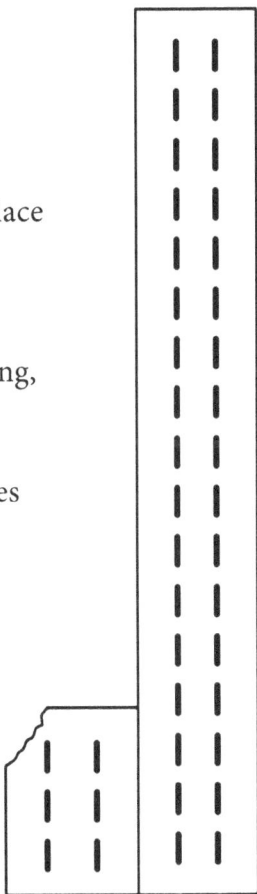

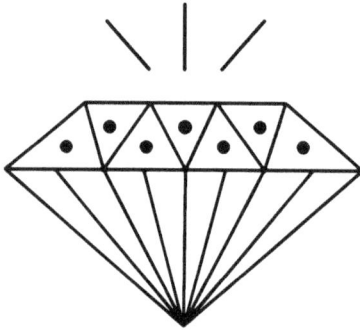

The bricks around her heart
were protecting
a delicate and sensitive diamond...

Empty days full of thoughts.
Filling nights with caustic shots.
Scouting for traces of a lonely body,
became an erratic, unsafe hobby.

The sheets twirl at the speed of light,
but on a list of ephemeral contacts,
she will never find a steady knight.

Forgotten in the streets of desperation,
drying her tears with the relieving tunes
of a distant radio station.

Clean your face
from your overprotective shield.
These gifts of yours
shouldn't remain sealed.

Give them to the ones
that need them most.
Share them with another heart.
Don't keep them closed...

You will always be lost
if you don't find yourself first.

I went everywhere,
but I couldn't find
home anywhere.

How could I
belong somewhere,
when I was constantly
feeling like a stranger
underneath my own skin...

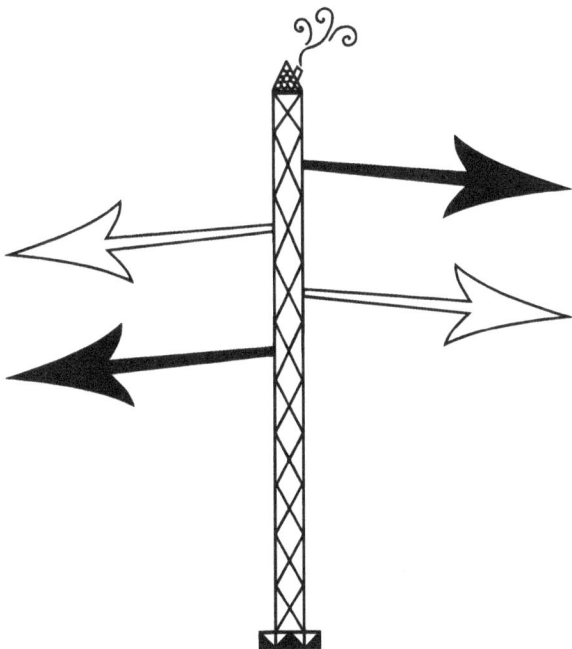

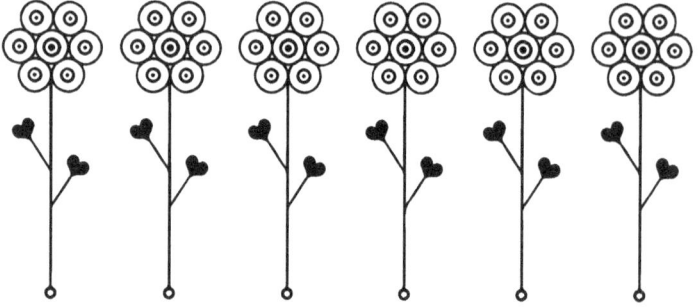

Don't sacrifice what you deserve
for what you want!

He left and your
face blanched
as he slammed
the door behind him.

You started crying
and eating
your emotions;
one bite after another,
trying to fill
the void of his absence.
One bite of anger.
One bite of sadness.
One bite of hate.
And finally, one bite of relief!
The last one was delicious,
wasn't it?

Please depart from planet "Grief"!

He left but was he ever there?
He left but you are still here!

As long as you've got yourself,
you've got everything.

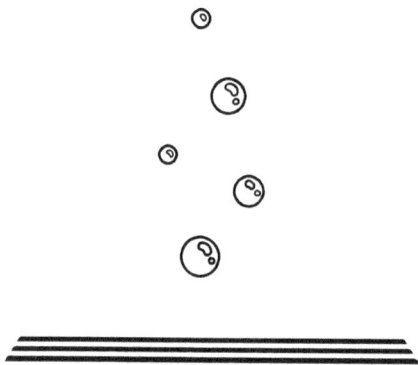

You won't find depth
in shallow waters...

The pillars looked
solid and firm,
but unfortunately
they were empty
and hollow inside.

How to start building
a roof on them,
when they couldn't even
hold the weight
of their own promises?

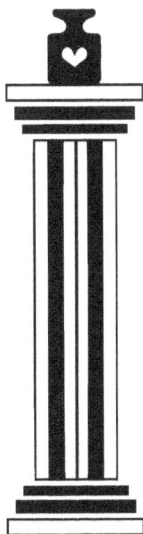

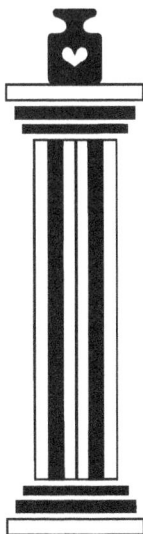

Your face is in total contrast
to your heart.

Your face is so beautiful.

I didn't let this volcano
of anger erupt
because I didn't want
to destroy you
or anyone;
until one day
it exploded inside
my chest and
destroyed me instead...

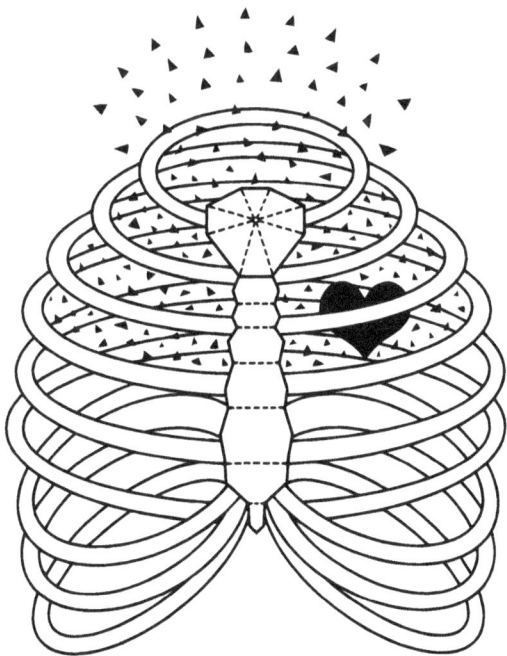

I kissed you and I tasted
the ugly flavor of your lies...

I was so thirsty
when I finally
saw an alluring jug
of water in front of me.

I quickly ran to get it;
I took it in my hands
and as I was ready
to drink it,
life came and spilled it
before it even
touched my lips.

And I got so mad
and furious and sad.

But then I looked closer
at that filthy liquid:
it was venom...

Thank you life,
for not always giving
me what I want.

Stop asking yourself
why did I fade away,
when you were the one who killed
this love with your own bare hands!

I invited you into my head,
but you vandalized this sacred place
and smeared its tranquility with
your infuriating, muddy boots.

Can you please move out of my mind?
You've become an undesirable tenant!

The time for you to leave has come.
No more chances. No more excuses.

Here's your eviction notice!
Now please let me escort you to
the door that you will never see open again!

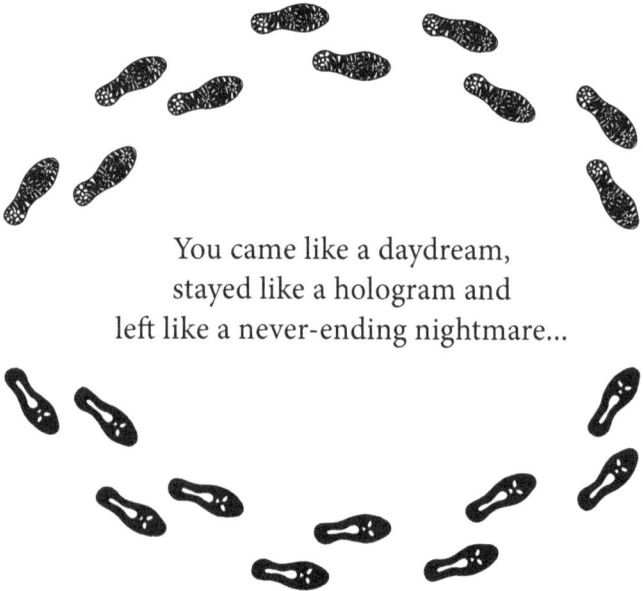

You came like a daydream,
stayed like a hologram and
left like a never-ending nightmare...

It was always... almost.
It was always so hard,
so painful,
so pointless.

Love seemed
so impossible for her;
impossible to find,
impossible to reach,
impossible to touch,
impossible to taste.

But her heart
was eagerly yearning
for its sweetness
every minute of the day
and every second of the night...

Excuse me,
but your mask fell off
and we can see the brutal face
of your real purpose.

Don't continue rehearsing
your despicable script.
The show is over now.

At the beginning,
he was like
a sentimental romantic
comedy.

Afterwards,
he changed the plot
into a horrible
tragedy.

Finally,
his awful acting
ended like
a grotesque
parody.

And then
the curtains fell
as she applauded
his disgraceful
performance,
with her ironic smirk
illuminating the stage,
but darkening his importance.

EGO

There wasn't a place for love
in your life
because it was already
too full of egotism!

You caused nothing but pain to me.

However, I took that raw pain
and transformed it into a gallery of shapes
and into a flood of words.

There will come the day
when my book will end up in your hands.
Be careful while you turn its pages.

My words are sharper than a sword
and you might get cut!

When I look at you now,
all I see is wasted time...

Your love had already expired
when you offered it to me.
And I knew it would be
dangerous for my health,
but I was so hungry
that I devoured it in one bite!

It turned my stomach upside down.
It infected my trust.
It smashed my tears.
It twisted my guts.

So I spit it out on burning papers!
I expunged it from my aching cells!
I flushed it down the drain
of hopeless fantasies,
until I found my cure in poetic spells...

My intuition was paralyzed by
his hesitant smile.

Who would have thought that
the innocence of his eyes
was a hideous abyss in disguise?

Who was he?
Why did he suddenly appear
in her life like a bitter curse
in a beautiful box?

Their bodies would never
sense the warmth of each other,
but their minds,
their minds were like
two powerful pylons
connected with invisible wires.

He couldn't hide from her.
She couldn't hide from him.
Who was he?
She didn't want an answer anymore.
She had cared too much.

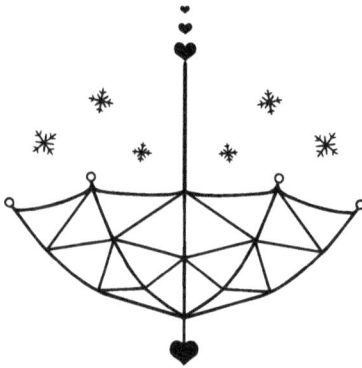

Your heart brings winter one day earlier...

Your words raped my soul.
They cut me so deep
that the wounds
are still open
after so many years.

My soul was young,
soft and happy,
but then it quickly died
like a colorless sunset
on a sad, rainy day.

When will these wounds heal?
I want my soul back!
Is there any piece of it still left
or am I searching for a decaying seed?

I have to get it back!
I owe it to the colors
that I dreamed
while it was still alive!

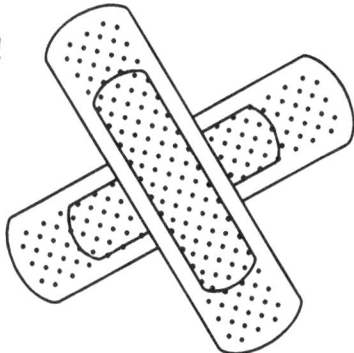

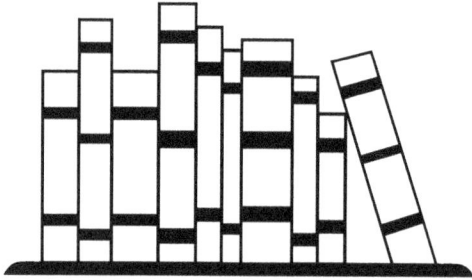

He only knew three words:
take, use, leave.

Give, love, stay,
didn't exist in his
fraudulent dictionary.

Thank you for your offer,
but no.
I am not interested
in the position
of part-time lover.

There is no room
for me here.
Such an overcrowded place!
The atmosphere
smells like sickness!

You can keep living
with your countless ghosts,
but you will never have
the privilege to corrupt
this divine body of mine!

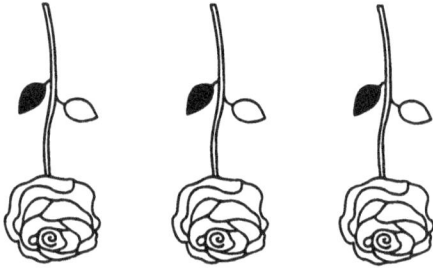

Don't kiss me anymore!
Don't touch me anymore!
Keep your hands away from me!
Your love has been tainted
and I don't want to be infected
by this obnoxious disease!

She could smell toxic souls
from miles away,
yet somehow she fell
in love with them.

She wanted to change them.
She felt the urge
to remove their toxins,
but their toxins couldn't disappear
unless they wanted to.
And they never wanted to...

So in the end,
she was the only one
who had changed.

And it was always for the worst...

Do you hear the deafening
sound of our silence?

The letter
that you never opened,
but threw it away
because its envelope
was strange,
torn and damaged,
was written
thousands of years ago
especially for you.

These kinds of letters
come once in a lifetime
and that rare one
had inside everything
you were looking for...

Love

letters

We come into this world alone
and we leave this world alone.
But we can be together in-between...

Parallel lives.
Divided worlds.

Let's start building
a bridge in the morning
and by the end of the day
our bodies will be tired
and our hands will be worn,
but our hearts will be beating
to the same, melodic rhythm...

He was powerful electricity
and she was potent water.

The intense current between them
was impossible to be unseen,
as it pervaded the atmosphere
like a thousand sparkling fireworks...

It was a love against the rules.
A love in unconventional motion.
No one could understand it.
They called them mad,
bizarre and
peculiar.

But love isn't born
to be understood anyway.

Love is here to be felt,
to be cherished,
to be praised.

Let the hearts that find love
celebrate it in all its glory!
They are the extremely blessed
and fortunate ones...

Let's escape from this deformed reality
for a while or forever...

My fear gently dies
as I get lost in
the constellations of your eyes.

Kiss my lips
with stellar light.
Set on fire
this moonless night.

Fill my lungs
with cosmic air.
Illuminate my body
with your final flare.

A galaxy that once
was so far away,
is now next to my heartbeat
and is here to stay.

In the deepest part of your soul;
there, you will find the answer.
In the deepest part of my soul;
there, I will find you...

Maybe
I wasn't sure,
maybe
you weren't too;
but our
older bones knew.

Like a dark winter
yearning
for the sunlight,
our bodies
were dragging us
to finally reunite...

Where are we going?
She asked.
To infinity and beyond!
He replied.

And they started running
through the endless poppy fields:
wild, free and invincible...

Under the sparkling stars,
lying next to each other,
they talked for hours
with only their curious eyes.

A long, intimate conversation,
until the moonlight
kissed them goodbye
and the night covered the sky
with her peaceful, warm blanket...

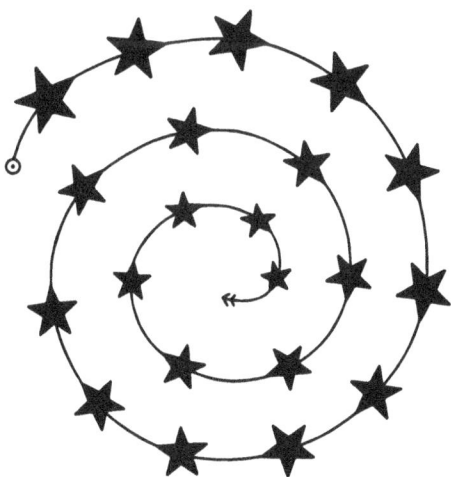

I love you

With my fingertip
I wrote those three words
in the burning sand.

But you will never read
them from where you stand.
Come closer...

Have we met before?
In the ballroom of a palace,
dancing our passion
on a blooming floor?

Have we met before?
Jumping from a pirate ship
and kissing on the shore?

Have we met before?
Hiding between the pages
of an old bookstore?

Have we met before?
My dear, I know we have.
And here we are, we met again
so we can love each other
a little bit harder and a little bit more.

Sometimes medicine comes
in the form of a pill.
Sometimes, it comes
in the form of a heart.

You will always be my irreplaceable remedy.
I will love you until the end of forever...

I can barely see your figure,
but I can hear every
single one of your words.

They are like a soft pillow
in an uncomfortable
bed of iron nails.

Like a breath of fresh air
in an asphyxiating room.

Like a sip of oasis
in the middle
of a deadly desert.

But the more I drink,
the thirstier I become.

Your words are my medicine,
addictive but healing medicine,
that start running through
my empty veins and
slowly fill me up
with drops of mythical,
everlasting life...

I wonder how many new dimensions
we could create together
if our minds collided
like an unstoppable, phenomenal explosion.

I believe our dominant blast
could even change
the direction of this world.

But we will never know.

I gravitate towards you,
but I can't break away from
the orbit of forbidden love.
You are my star and
I can admire you only from afar...

It was a planet of fire.
For the adventure, desire.
A puzzle of dreams
between bluebirds and streams.

It was her own planet.
Her heart was like a magnet.
A warm and safe nest,
where bruised souls
could rest.

A cloudless sky,
so far and so high.
Open for few
and mostly for you...

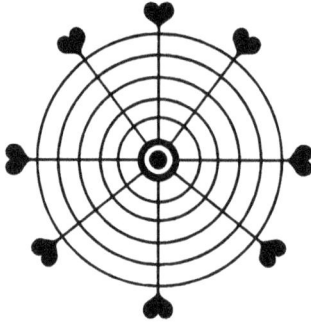

I sit next to you,
but you are miles away.
My mind tells me to go,
but my heart wants to stay.

I know there is nothing I can do.
I'm so afraid to leave this room.
But no matter how much I try,
I can't make
a withered rose bloom...

Nowadays love
has become like
a fast food meal:
fast, cheap, easy and unhealthy.

Is this love
or is this a low-quality substitute
to replenish the deserted
bedrooms of your loneliness?

A healthy love requires
the finest ingredients:
honesty, trust,
compromise, respect.
Stir them passionately
until your hearts have absorbed
all these essential
elements to the fullest!

Great things take time.

Something rushed
will satisfy your cravings just
for the halftime of indigent nights.

Something prepared with
patience and pure love
will indulge your soul for a lifetime...

?

If not here then where?
If not now then when?
If not you then who?

Questions floating in the fog,
searching for answers
in the remote islands of hidden desires...

Where are you, my love?
It's already Fall o'clock.

Winter is just
around the corner
and I'm longing for
your gentle touch
to keep me warm.

And winter came,
but you never did.

The cold was piercing
my bones,
but the thought of you
kept my pulse alive
inside my numb,
frozen body...

Wake up! You deserve to be adored...

You should never
feel lonely,
unwanted
and rejected.
I love you, he said.

And her heavy,
troubled world
stopped turning
for a second...

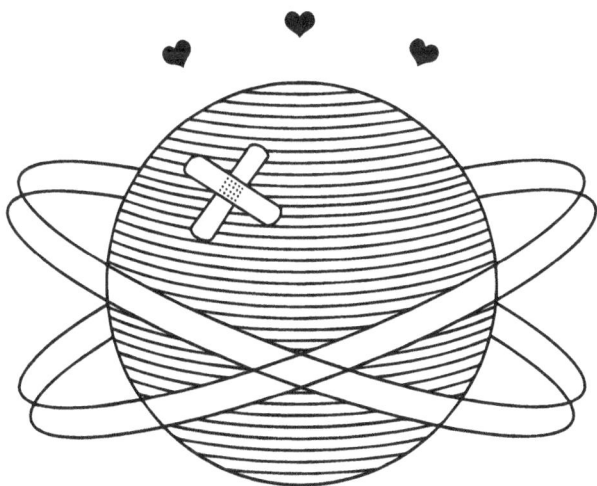

Meet me in our secret place
beyond the horizon;
where you first saw my naked soul,
where I first dived in the clarity of your eyes,
where we left our love unsaid.

Time to finish what we never started...

Strangely familiar footprints.
A poisonous passage.
A clear skyline.
A fiery stare.
A smile.
You...

I found
a hidden gem
in the ethereal charm
of your existence
and my life never
looked more splendid.

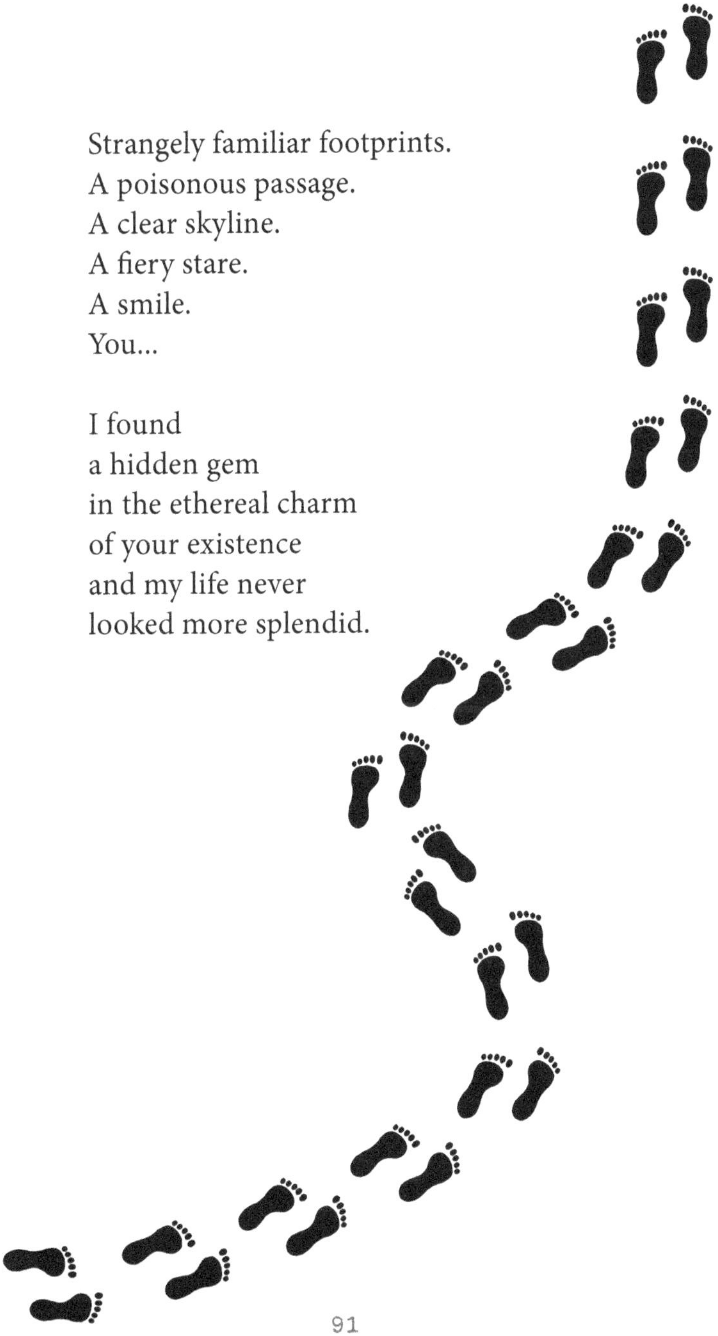

I hate you so much,
but I love you more.

Someone help me understand
this complicated oxymoron...

You told me that there are
different types of love.
Love out of convenience.
Love out of loneliness.
Love out of boredom.
Love out of interest.
Love out of routine.
Love out of fear.

You have no idea what love is.

Love is risky!
Love is crazy!
Love is honest!
Love is intense!
Love is passionate!
Love is spontaneous!
Love is unconditional!

Don't call anything
less than this "love".

You're offending the word!

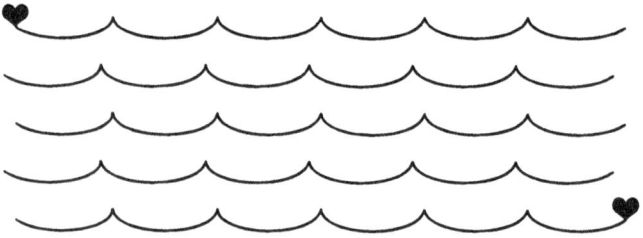

Waves crashing on the shore
And my mind is starting a war

I hug the sky and I kiss the sea
But you're not here, next to me

There will come a day
when you will understand
that love is like walking on a tightrope,
without a safety net underneath.

Some will fall.
Some will jump.

But true love is for the brave ones!
True love is for the ones who dare!

For those who
dare to leave the ground
and walk in the air
just to meet each other
in the middle
despite the distractions
and the weight of
the world around them!

And then,
you will remember me,
but it will be too late...

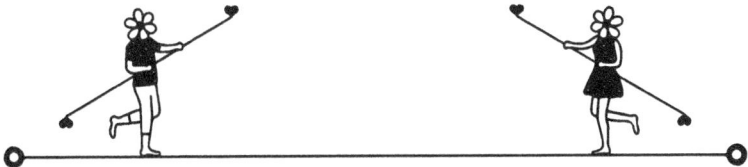

We're just temporary travelers
in this colossal, astral dust...

You are still here.

In the tenderness of your touch.
In the warmth of your hugs.
In the echoes of your laughter.
In the softness of your kiss.

In the wisdom of your mind.
In the beauty of your words.
In the melody of your voice.
In the light of your smile.

You are still here.
Still living right next to my heart.

Until we meet again...

Self-love

letters

Only the persistent ones will reach the top!

It was true.
She was like a river.
She was always flowing:
down mountains,
through valleys,
along plains.

Sculpting and transforming
herself through the journey.
Crashing into rocks and glaciers,
but quickly recovering and
moving forward again.

She didn't want to be
stagnant water.
That kind of water
is worse than poison.
She wanted to develop,
to evolve,
to grow.

Dark dams tried
to stop her,
but little did they know.

No one could stop her but herself!

Her fairy tales never had a happy ending;
until she decided that
she should be the one who holds
both the pencil and the rubber.

I trusted my happiness in trembling hands.
They let it fall and it shattered
into a thousand, painful pieces.

I trusted my happiness in angry hands.
They strangled its innocence
until its last gasp of terror.

I trusted my happiness in confused hands.
They lost it in a tangled forest
of insecurities.

I trusted my happiness in filthy hands.
They made me feel sick of
my skin and they laughed
as I ripped my flesh in disgust.

I trusted my happiness in my own hands.
The first, little rosebud of joy
started blooming in my tired smile,
after a long, exhausting time…

I will find the right materials.
I will learn the skills.
I will gain the strength.

I can rebuild myself!
I can and I will!

Oh, there it is again!
Another trick of yours
disguised as love!

I'm sorry, but I can't
allow it this time.
My feelings are under construction.

I AM AN ARTWORK IN PROGRESS!

I'm a canvas ready
to sense the caress
of new, delightful brushstrokes.

Please keep out!
I need fresh paint and
you are just a dry stain!

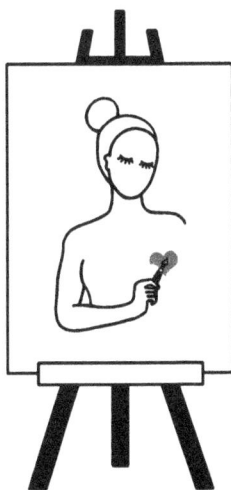

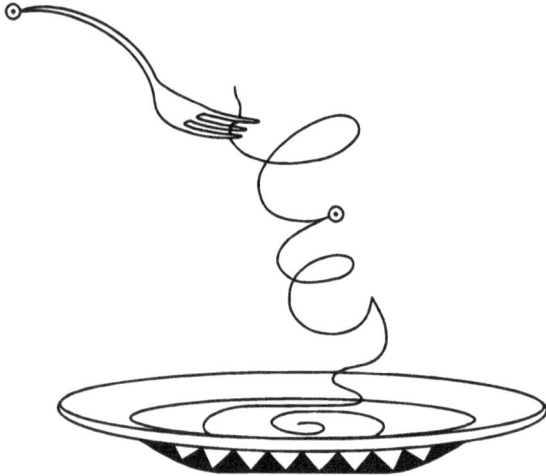

Don't digest what you're given on the plate.

Taste it first and spit it
if you don't like the flavor!

Your wound is never
going to heal
if you keep scraping
it with that knife!

Trust me.
Put the knife down
and give me your hand.

You're not alone anymore...

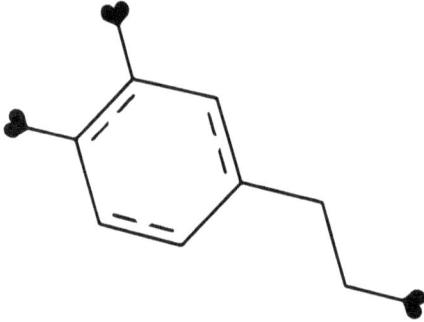

She was made of
gold and steel.
She was not afraid to love
and she was not afraid to feel.

A big heart is not a sign of weakness.
It is a sign of exceptional,
undaunted boldness!

I had survived!

Completely wrapped
in layers of
disturbing marks
that reminded me
each and every one
of my horrific struggles.

But I had survived
and I was being born
for a second time...

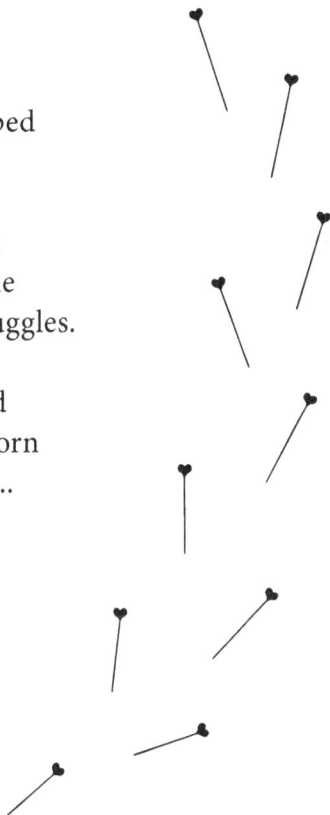

Breathe in a wave of salty wind.
Breathe out all your worries, child...

Two crystal tears
ran down her face.

A sad one,
for everything that
yesterday took away.
A happy one,
for everything that
today brought along.

Those crystals were
like time machines
streaming on their
lucid screens
her days,
her nights,
her dreams,
her fights.

And there she was,
washing her old consciousness
from the dirt of crooked imagery
and wearing a new veil
of radical metamorphosis.

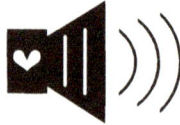

Mute the noise around you
and listen to your inner voice.
Listen carefully and then
follow the way it's telling you to follow.

And on this way
there will be supporters,
but there will be enemies, too.
Don't let the last ones affect you.
Let them drown in their own malice.

Keep listening and
following your voice.
As long as your heart is at peace,
the noise around you
will sound like calming music.

She felt so small;
smaller than
a drop of rain.

But then she remembered
her mother's words:
the majesty of the ocean
doesn't make a tiny pearl less precious.

It's a wonderful,
unique miracle created
within this tremendous,
blue world
and so are you...

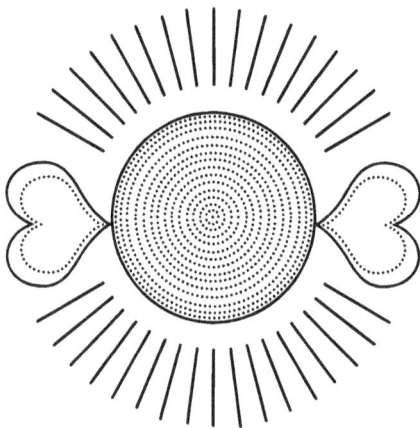

The sun after the blizzard
is the sweetest sun.

Don't give up now
that you tripped on
the first rocks
of your self-doubt.

Don't give up now
that you felt
the harsh miscarriage
of your plans.

Don't give up now
that the birds of regret
are furiously flying
above your confused head.

Don't give up now
that you have walked
through hell
to reach this sky.

Don't give up now
that everything is blurry.
The sun sets, but it rises again!

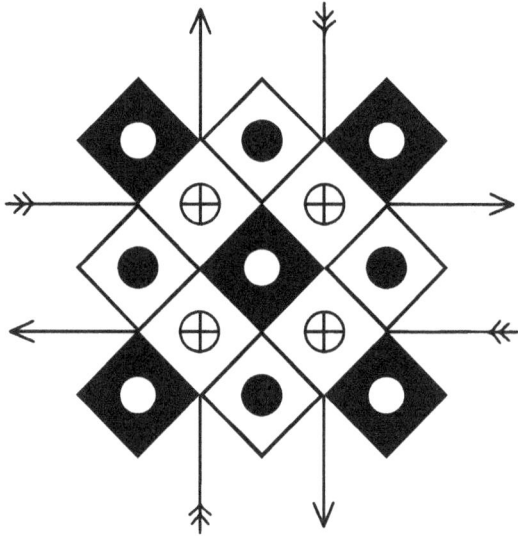

Excellence scares the ones
who are used to mediocrity.

You weren't created to be approved.
You already carry the sublime beauty
of the universe in your vessels.

You weren't created to fit in molds.
Build yourself inside your own,
unique and incomparable cocoon.

You weren't created to be ignored.
Don't be afraid to raise your voice
at those who trample on your flowers.

You were created with a heart.
Hearts work better
when they exchange love...

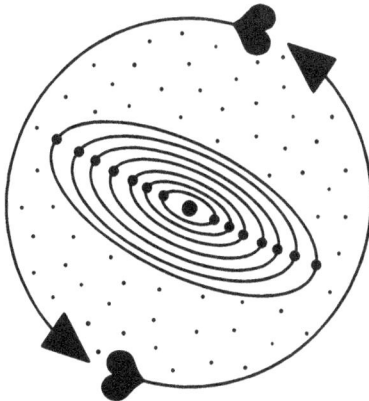

We can't stay the same.
We must grow in life, sweetheart.
In order to grow, we must change.
And change is difficult,
but so beautiful and
redemptive at the same time.

Don't fear change,
fear stagnation.

Stagnation is a slow, horrific torture.

The little boat
never left that shore.
Year after year,
it just stayed anchored
to that old, destroyed harbor,
dissolving day by day,
afraid of what life could be
behind the big mountain.

You have to break the chains
that keep you enslaved
to this illusion of withered safety!
You have to sail away!
Shouted its inner voice.

But the little boat
didn't want to listen.
So it continued to stay
around its familiar waters,
until it finally sank:
rusty, empty and neglected...

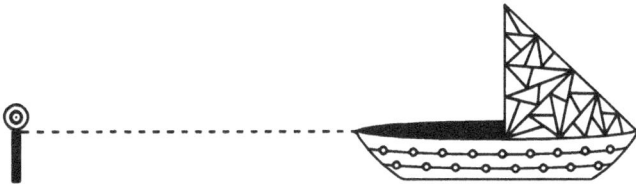

Don't ask a spoiled,
indoor narcissus for life advice.
Ask a wildflower.

They cut her wings,
but she didn't fall.
They couldn't touch
her fearless soul.

You can't destroy a heart
when it ignites.
Eagles soar through storms
to reach greater heights!

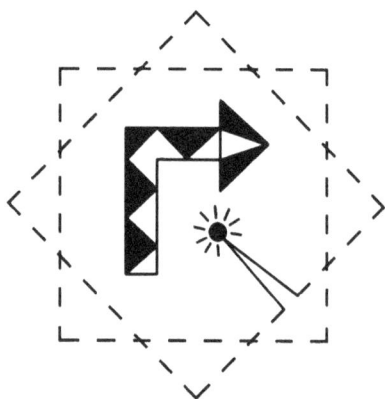

It's never too late to right your wrongs...

I fell and broke my dreams.
My heart told me to keep going.

I slipped and hurt my patience.
My heart told me to keep going.

I reached the distant point
where the Sun meets the Darkness
and bravely conquers it!

My heart beamed
in an ecstasy
of ultimate fulfillment...

When "nothing" is placed
under the spotlight,
people will start believing
that "nothing" is "something".
Eventually, "nothing" will start believing
that it's "something" too
and it's all downhill from there...

You are afraid of solitude
because you tremble
at the idea of
being alone with
your worst enemy:
yourself.

I seek solitude
so I can be alone
with my best friend:
myself.

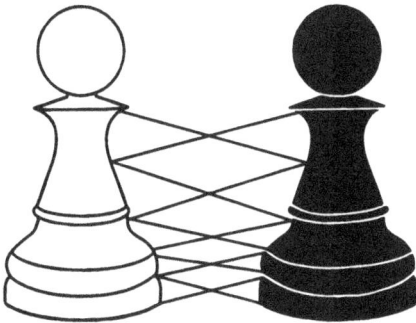

The obvious is difficult
to be seen by the eyes
when the mind is obstinately
stuck to an incorrect estimation.

What a priceless treasure
that you are!
How lucky will be the ones
that will hold your rich intelligence
and your breathtaking psyche
in their arms.

You are a lot,
but some hands
can barely
carry a little.

Don't downgrade
your wonderful traits
so you can fit in
small, ungrateful palms.

Spread your magic
beyond the boundaries
of narrow hearts.
Grow and glow fearlessly!

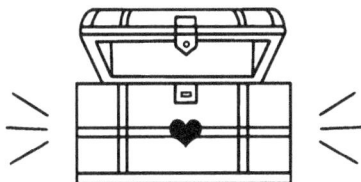

Don't underestimate me so easily.
Tiny spikes can overturn big trucks!

They told her she was a girl
and they meant that she was weak.
She should just agree and listen,
but she should never speak.

She should give them her crown
and always keep her head down.
She should never walk alone at night
and she should never fight.

The princess that they mocked
for wearing a cotton candy dress,
was smarter than all of them
and braver than a lioness.

She broke their idiotic rules
and instead, she wrote more books
because only the power of education
can eliminate the fools!

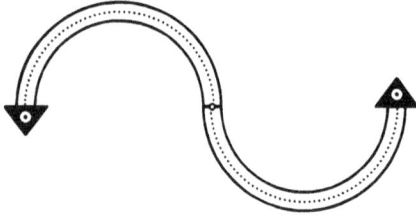

Someone who continually
contradicts themselves,
is not a trustworthy person.

They are showing you
their true nature
right before your eyes!
Why do you still insist on seeing them
as a delightful dream?

Wake up from your hallucinations darling
and see the facts that are screaming
in front of you!
You won't find the missing part of
honesty on a mount of mendacity!

Your love is like the fresh snow;
it comes only during your winters.
It looks beautiful and playful,
but it quickly melts
as soon as I try to touch it.

Love shouldn't be like this.
Love shouldn't make you feel
like you're waiting in a long line
to buy tickets for a bus that
is never going to arrive anyway.

Love shouldn't make you feel
like a beggar, waiting for
a few crumbs of affection.

This is not love.
I don't want it.
I refuse it...

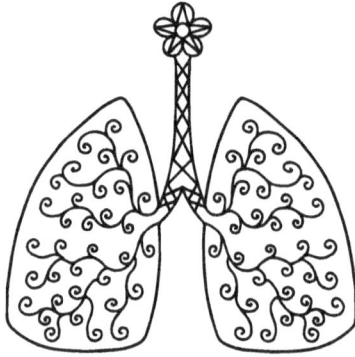

I cried when you left the room...
They were tears of joy!

I had forgotten the sensation of clear oxygen
in my drained lungs.

Once, I was weak.
Once, I believed the beautifully
crafted words of the wind,
but then I realized they were
just immature words
drifting in the air.

Words without a serious meaning,
words without a purpose,
words that got me tired,
words that I didn't want to hear anymore.

They could lift me up into the sky
for a little while and at the same time
they would let me collapse on the ground,
having no compunction at all.

Now the only thing I believe
is the strength of my own willpower.
Now I am the only one
who decides my direction in the sky.
Now I am unbreakable!

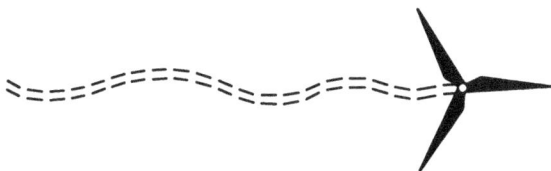

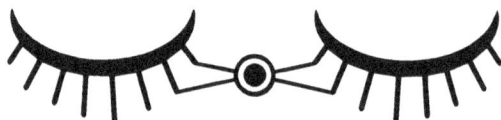

It's not easy being woke
in a society where people
are sleeping with their eyes open.

Look at them.
Same clothes.
Same hair.
Same faces.
No brains.

Look at them.
Doing what they are told to do.
Eating what they are told to eat.
Wearing what they are told to wear.
Seeing what they are told to see.
Feeling what they are told to feel.
Saying what they are told to say.
Thinking what they are told to think.

Like a legion of breathing zombies!
What a disgraceful,
synchronized parade...

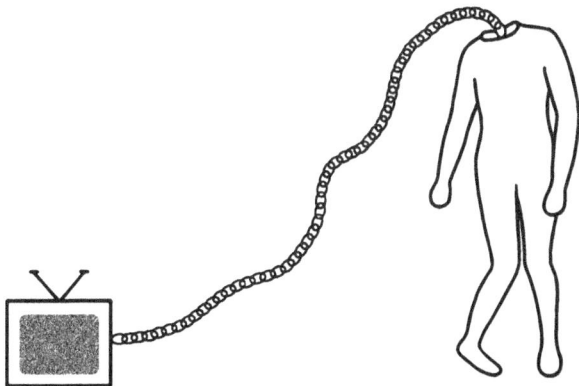

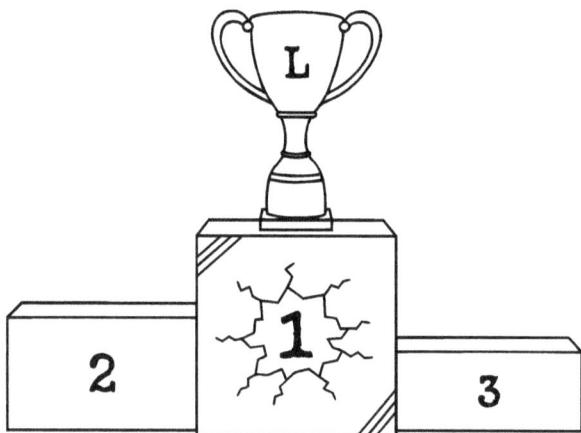

A deceitful win is twice a failure!

Don't expect everyone
to share the same morals as you
or everyone to respect fair play.

There are people who won't
hesitate to break the rules
in order to reach their goal.

And they will steal the cup
from your clean hands,
but don't get disappointed.

As history and time have proven,
achievements based on
deceptive foundations
collapse and crash down
like weak sand podiums.

Call it a well-deserved
boomerang from life...

Manipulative people will always
find a fake excuse for their actions
when they get caught.
They have an answer ready for everything.
They are the losers who can't achieve
anything in an ethical way.

After all, they are good
at one thing only:
playing mind games.

If you enjoy playing with people's lives,
please notice that in these games,
the only loser is you!

I hadn't done anything wrong to them.
They just couldn't stand the fact
that my spirit was shinier than theirs.

So, they tried to throw dirty soil at me.
I took it, I cleaned it and I planted
glorious, red roses in it.

They tried to bury me alive
in their evil, irrational rage.
I raised my radiant rays above them
even higher than before.

In the end, all their plans
to demolish my indomitable spirit,
automatically turned against them.

They got trapped in their own snares
and they tripped over
their own malicious hurdles
that unethically had prepared for me.

And I watched this satisfying
final episode of their paranoia,
while enjoying a nice bottle of justice
in my lovely garden of roses...

You put a joker on a throne
and then wonder
why your life is ruled by a fool!

I had warned you
not to mess with swamps,
hadn't I girl?

You got so lost in it,
you almost became one too.
Don't ever forget that you are a river
and rivers aren't supposed to stay still!

They move.
They explore.
They get lost.
They discover!

You need a vivid river
just like you to wander with
and not a rotten swamp, my dear.

So, go!
Don't stop!
Always keep flowing!
You're in the right direction now!

Their insanity
was affecting my sanity
until I found my antidote in art.

I'm spinning like a crazy ball
in my life's roulette.
Where am I going to land?
I don't know yet.

Life keeps hitting me
on igneous rocks.
I feel trapped in this
downhill spiral of paradox.

I've lost control.
My heart's turning into ice.
Is it too late now
to roll the dice?

I can do it,
I can define my own way.
I can do it
and I will start today!

Pay attention to their shadows, my dear.
Don't just look at their lighted side...

If you could see
what you don't see,
you would see that
what you see
is what they want you to see
and sometimes what you want to see.

Throw those blinders away from your face!

Unless you find
limited vision convenient.
Then just sit back and
enjoy the counterfeit view!

You are surrounded by
all these cruel voices,
shouting that you won't make it!

Hush them up with the loud sound
of your success!

Those eyes are starving
for your failure.
Those eyes are haunting you.
They are waiting
for you to collapse,
in order to majestically
turn on their "I told you so"
neon light sign and chant
the refrains of a sick celebration.

Oh, shut up Mr. and Mrs. "know it all"
because you know nothing!

You don't know
how my life ignites
every time I mention
my dream's name.

You don't know
how many miles
I have walked
to ascend this
steep hill of hopeless
and hopeful stairs.

You sit, look, judge,
but you know nothing!

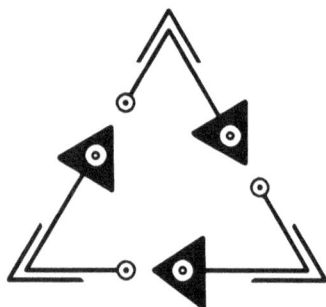

If you want to have
a new, better life,
you have to stop recycling
your old, bad habits.

You always adjust your colors
according to your surroundings.

But after changing so many
costumes in your life,
you lost sight of
your true self.

You are afraid
that nobody will like
what is hidden underneath
your ostentatious clothes.

Why don't you show
for once in your life,
who you really are,
your naked personality,
with its marks, its scars,
its remarkable beauty, its true colors!
The colors that only I can see
under all these fancy,
unnecessary fabrics...

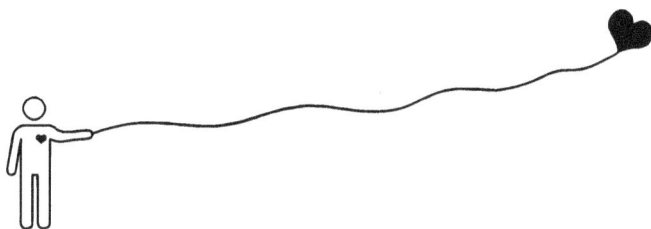

People seem to grow up
and leave their hearts behind them...

Your value isn't found
in the wealth around you.
It's found in the wealth WITHIN you!

I won't ask you
if you are proud
of the things you have.

I will ask you
if you are proud
of the person you have become.

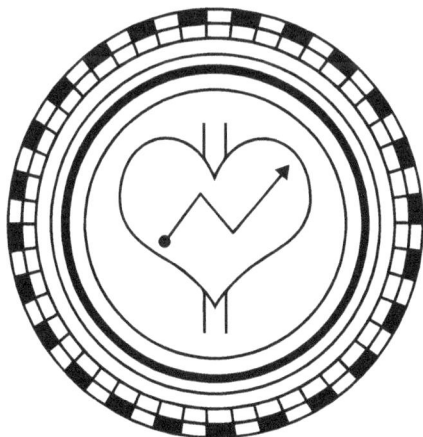

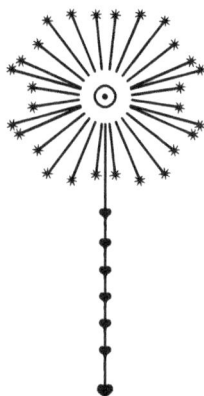

Oh, but what would I be
without my dreams?
Just a bunch of flesh and bones.

I know that one day
the Impossible will triumph over
the Possible and the flames of my work
will turn into magical dust...

It's better to go with
all your heart after
what you really want,
desire,
dream,
than to settle down
to a mediocre,
but easy solution.

Maybe you won't
achieve your goal,
but this doesn't mean
that you have failed.

The one who does not try at all,
is the one who has already failed.

The acts of today
will hunt you down tomorrow, too.

Will they fondle
or will they sting?
That depends on you...

If I pretended what I feel
I'd fool myself and never heal
Winter's tears or laughter's spring
What I feel is real

Always being myself
There is no net to catch my soul
It goes only where it wants to be
But open to give it all

Never afraid of taking chances
I don't want the day to pass me by
Cause if I was afraid of flying
I'd still be crawling on thorny ground

I won't be my own hedge
There are no limits on a razor's edge
I'm going to fall and fly again
As long as my wings can stand the pain

Choose carefully where you trust your life.

If you keep holding on to a broken branch,
sooner or later,
you're going to fall and break yourself!

Could they overcome
the obstacles
that were blocking them
from reaching each other?

He could,
but he didn't.
She couldn't,
but she did.

And at that moment
she knew
he wasn't the one
worth fighting for...

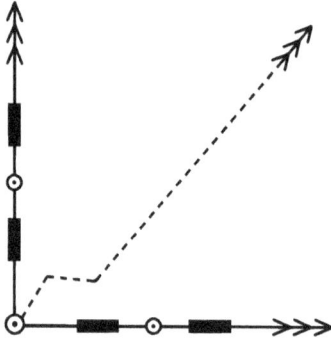

Person A has 5 apples,
which he got from the apple tree
he planted in his backyard.
Person B has 50 apples,
which he stole from person A's tree.
The moral of my little story:
don't pay so much attention to what people have.
Pay attention to WHO they are and
to HOW they got what they have!

If you want maximal results
with minimal and sneaky effort, remember:
The fruits of deception
will stick in your throat one day!

I had to eat a million
failed attempts,
before taking a small
bite of success.

I had to swim in
an ocean of despair,
before reaching
the first step of progress.

I had to climb
a mountain of sacrifices,
before arriving at the peak
of my resistance.

You think I just clapped
my hands and things
effortlessly went my way.

You're wrong.

I have paid with
countless anxious days
and endless sleepless nights
everything I have achieved in my life.

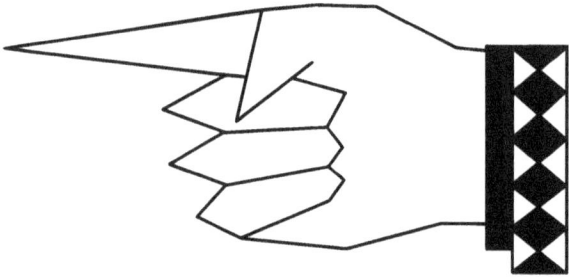

I almost fell for you,
but thankfully I noticed the credibility gap
between your insincerity and your fake integrity
and I didn't stumble.

You can fool everyone
else around you,
but you can't fool me, she said.

You're just another surface lover!
Nothing more, nothing new!

Staying for too long
on the surface
makes me nauseous,
she continued while breaking
the ice with her fist and diving
into the vast and profound
mystery of the Unknown.

And he got mad at her
because she cracked
his delusive reflections...

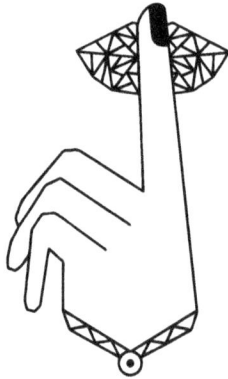

Let's take a moment of silence
for those who confuse
confidence with arrogance!

I started growing
when I decided
to cut all the weed
around me.

I was motionless
and I couldn't evolve
because they were stealing
all of my energy,
light and space.

Although it's not easy
to get rid of these
merciless invaders,
tear their roots
with determination
and sow your personal
mission and
your own vision
in their place.

You will see how
far you will go
once you clean
your territory
from hostile raiders.

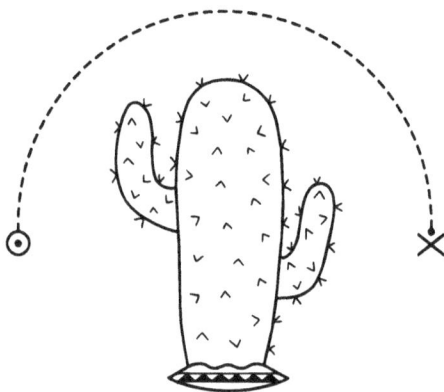

I want + fear = I won't

The fear of the new path.
The fear that makes you
turn down a journey without
trying it first.
It was only her diffidence
standing in front of her.

But opportunities don't wait for you.
They appear in a flash
and disappear in the blink of an eye.
Only the bold and the quick ones have
the privilege to enjoy these valuable chances.

So, she jumped over the high fence
of her hesitation
and landed on the other
side of the risk.

And she was so thrilled
to find out that
the new path was the right one...

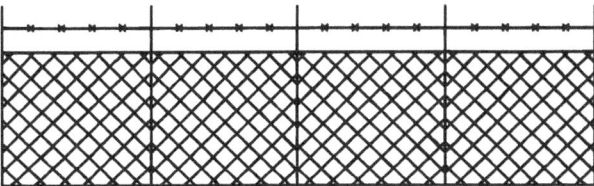

You felt so threatened
by my brilliant flame
that you kept throwing
angry water to put it out.

But angry water doesn't
always extinguish a fire.
Sometimes it causes
an even bigger burst than before.

Watch out!
You might get burned this time!

Like a sneaky fisherman,
they throw their tainted bait
and patiently wait for
your reaction.

Don't interact with
these kinds of baits
because that's exactly
what they seek.

Even a bit of your attention
will add undeserved value
to these wily,
walking failures.

Don't feed the mouth
that is hungry for
your extermination.

Open your eyes,
open your ears,
but be wise enough to know
what to let in and what to avoid.

Ignore ignorance, my friend.

Don't ever implore anyone to love you.

Love should unfold naturally.
Love should never be forced.

Cuffed hearts won't stay
together for too long.
One of them will break the chain
and the other will break to pieces...

If you want to come into my life,
come in an hour earlier.

If you want to leave my life,
leave two hours earlier.

You can stay as long as
your feet are clean.
You can enter the gate
only once though.
You can leave,
but you can't
come back in.

Attention!
Once your feet get dirty,
they aren't allowed to cross
my spotless threshold anymore.

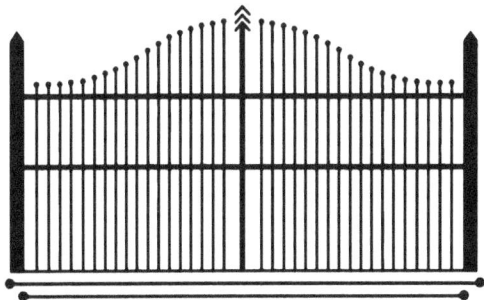

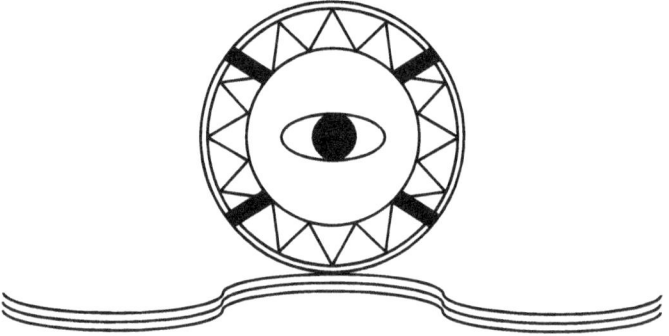

The truth is like a life jacket.
You can try to hide
and push it in the water,
but it will always come back
to the surface!

ALWAYS!

It's all in or all out!
All in? Great!
All out? It's fine again.

Don't ever consume
yourselves in sick situations
of annoying, emotionally
immature babies
living in adult bodies!

You don't need them.
They are giving you
nothing but
pending questions
and uncertain answers.

Release your life from
their needy whining
and their indecisive
inner conflicts.

Don't wait for them
to grow up,
while letting yourself
to ungracefully grow old.

While you are worrying about
what they are thinking of you,
they are worrying about
what you are thinking of them.

I admit it.
The greatest saboteur of my life was me.

A noxious mixture
of fears and tears
was pulling me down
in a numb lethargy.

The road to your dreams is hard,
but it's harder to live
with a heavy "what if" on your
shoulders for the rest of your life.

You have to move,
you have to sail against the wind,
the circumstances will never be perfect...

You will live a rich life
only if you constantly polish it
with love, affection and kindness.

You must fit in, to be accepted!
If you don't fit in,
then you'll be an unwanted outcast
living in the peripheral
sides of our circle.
Nobody will care about you
if you don't look perfect!
Flaws are not accepted here,
so if you don't look like us
you are not welcomed,
they said.

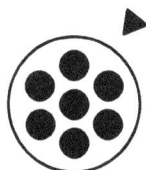

I've met a lot of unattractive people
with attractive faces!
I don't want to look like all of you.
What does "perfect" mean anyway?
I like being unique in a world
that is trying so hard to make me
a "perfect" copy-paste by forcing me
to obey dehumanizing standards.
I don't want to fit in your freakish molds!
I shouted and I saw their power over me
decrease until they completely disappeared
and couldn't harm me anymore...

You see, their power grows
only if your insecurities grow.
The more you love yourself,
the quicker they'll become insignificant.

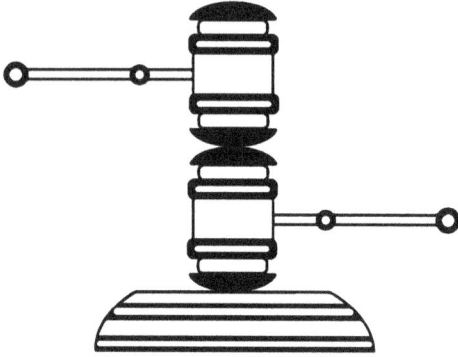

How ironic!
Immoral judges dare
to criticize your life!

Don't listen to them.

This is not constructive love,
this is destructive hate.
And hate can never heal, it can only kill.

If you want to stop something,
stop it TODAY!
If you want to start something,
start it TODAY!
If you want to do something,
do it TODAY!
If you want to tell her you love her,
tell her TODAY!

What?
There's no hurry to take the initiative?

Here's a glass of mortality
to help you swallow your pride.

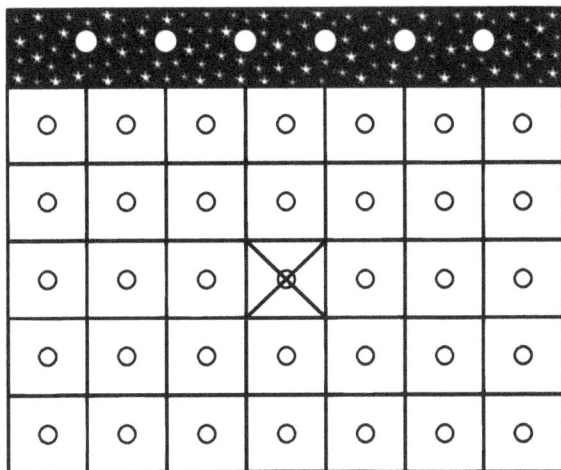

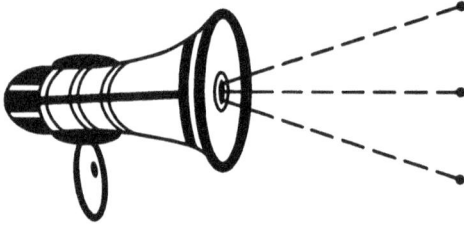

They might not believe you.
They might laugh.
They might try to blame you.

The evil knows how to hide
behind masks
and behind of silence.

No more silence!

SHOUT the truth to the world
with EVERY SINGLE cell of your body!

Shout it LOUD until the day
it finally gets heard!

Every time you drop
a stone into this lake,
it forms a series of ripples
which affect the living creatures
around them.

Think before using your stones
and make sure to throw them
only if you have good intentions.

This lake is your life
and the stones you are holding
are your words and actions, kid...

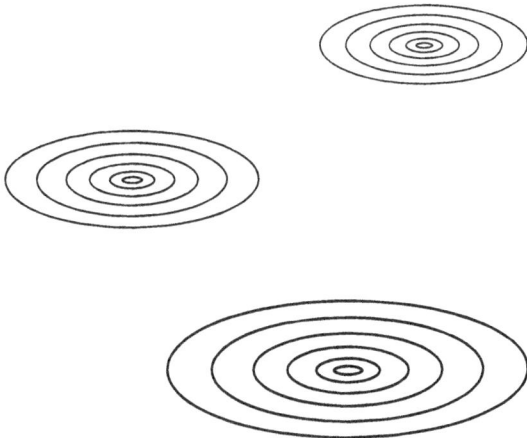

We can be divided
or we can choose to be united.

We live under the same sky
and on the same land!

Don't ever forget that...

Art has no borders.
Creativity has no borders.
Friendship has no borders.
Love has no borders.
In reality, there are no borders
at all on this planet.
Mankind decided to cut this land
to pieces and give them different names.
How much blood has been shed for a few
meters of ground to have a different name?
It's unbelievable, isn't it?

There are no borders.
The only borders that exist
are those around a closed mind.
A mind stuck on prejudice.
A mind that hates for no reason.
You might not have chains on your hands,
but you will never be free
if you keep your mind in chains.
Be open to learning.
Be open to embrace
someone different than you.
Revamp your heart.
Upgrade your mindset.

Don't show me the easy,
convenient road.
I won't follow it!

What is the point
of following a road
that is going to teach me
what I already know?

My time is limited
and I can't spend it in a
predictable direction.

I don't care
what everyone else
expects from me!

I can't ignore my soul
when it's demanding
to chase its missing parts.

I can't pretend.
I can't betray myself...

I need to go off-road.

This way,
I will see the world
from a different
pair of eyes.

This way,
I will listen to
a kind of music
unfamiliar to my ears.

This way,
I will walk barefoot
on the corners of
undiscovered lands.

This way,
I will learn how to dance
in a stranger's shoes.

This way,
I will feel peaceful,
complete and revived...

Afraid to try
Afraid to lose
Afraid to laugh
Afraid to choose

You wake up, but you're still sleeping
You don't talk, but you are screaming
You start running, but where are you going?
You're walking faster, but you are crawling

Toxic blood explodes your veins
Your rainbow soul fights rusty chains
A black cloud sits on your shoulder
Your confused thoughts need a decoder

It's a fast, fast life
You've got to give me your hand
It's a never-ending strife
But I'm here my friend

It's a fast, fast life
But by the end of the day
Are you the hunter or the prey?
It's a fast, fast life

You live in the shadow
Because you're afraid of light
You drink a color
But it's never bright

And in this strange
Methystic atmosphere
You're seeing notes
But you can't hear

It's a fast, fast life
So wait! You have to slow down!
Before three clock hands
Steal your precious crown

It's a fast, fast life
I see it in your brilliant, rainy eyes
You're ready now
You're ready for new skies

My friend, don't be afraid
Unlock your mind and open the doors
Because all this world of mine
All this world is yours

This seems like

The End

but this is just the beginning...